Lise Meitner

Published in the United States of America by Cherry Lake Publishing
Ann Arbor, Michigan
www.cherrylakepublishing.com

Content Adviser: Jessica Criales, Doctoral Candidate, History Department, Rutgers University
Reading Adviser: Marla Conn MS, Ed., Literacy specialist, Read-Ability, Inc.
Book Design: Jennifer Wahi
Illustrator: Jeff Bane

Photo Credits: ©Irina Papoyan/Shutterstock, 5; ©spiber.de/Shutterstock, 7; ©Tupungato/Shutterstock, 9, 22;
©PD-1923, 11; ©PD-1923, 13; ©Everett Historical/Shutterstock, 15; ©Grasko/Shutterstock, 17, 23; ©KREML/
Shutterstock, 19; ©Science History Image / Alamy Stock Photo, 21; Cover, 8, 12, 16, Jeff Bane; Various frames
throughout, ©Shutterstock Images

Library of Congress Cataloging-in-Publication Data has been filed and is available at catalog.loc.gov

Printed in the United States of America
Corporate Graphics

About the author: Sara Spiller is a native of the state of Michigan. She enjoys reading comic books and hanging out with her cats. She wants to help empower people all over the world, including women scientists.

About the illustrator: Jeff Bane and his two business partners own a studio along the American River in Folsom, California, home of the 1849 Gold Rush. When Jeff's not sketching or illustrating for clients, he's either swimming or kayaking in the river to relax.

I was born in Austria in 1878.
My family was Jewish.

I loved math. But girls could not go to school with boys.

I was **tutored**. My father wanted his daughters to learn.

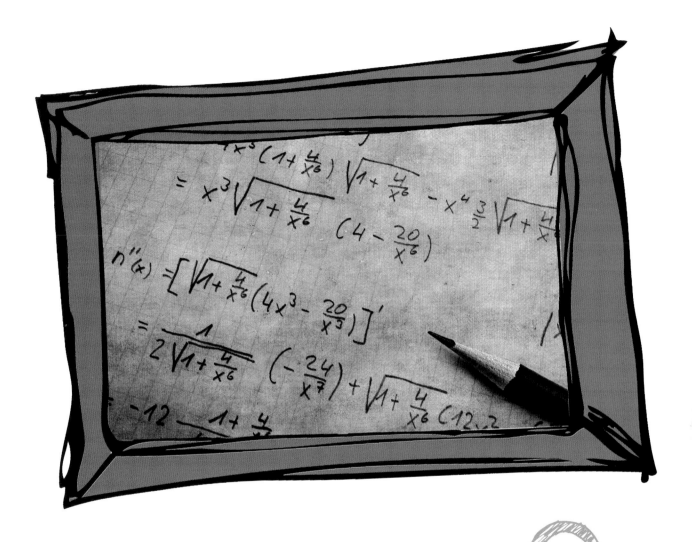

Why is it good for girls to learn?

I studied **physics**. I earned a **doctorate** from my school.

I was the second woman to do this.

I did **research**. The men I worked with were unfair to me.

I was not paid for my work.

What do you do when you see unfairness?

I worked with Otto Hahn.
We did tests. We made
discoveries.

There was a war. The German army came into my country.

Jews were in danger. I had to escape.

I went to live in Sweden.

I made a discovery. **Atoms** could split and make **energy**!

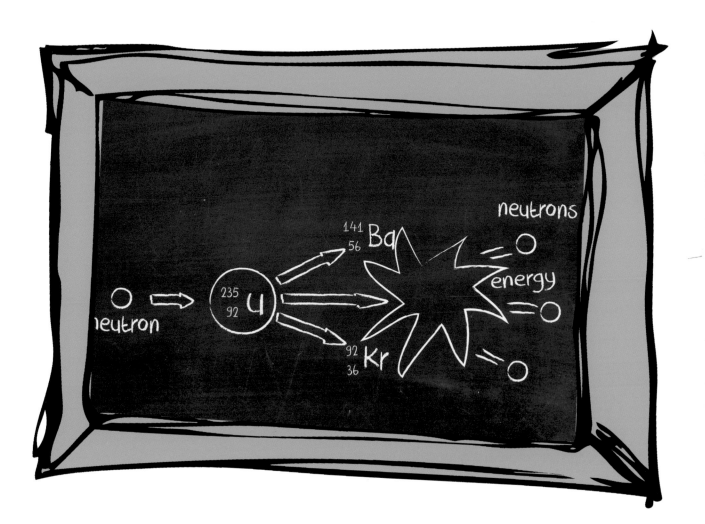

I became well-known. But people made **weapons** with this energy.

I did not want to make weapons.

When do you disagree with others?

I died in 1968. I showed others that girls are smart. I led the way.

What would you like to ask me?

1906

1870

Born
1878

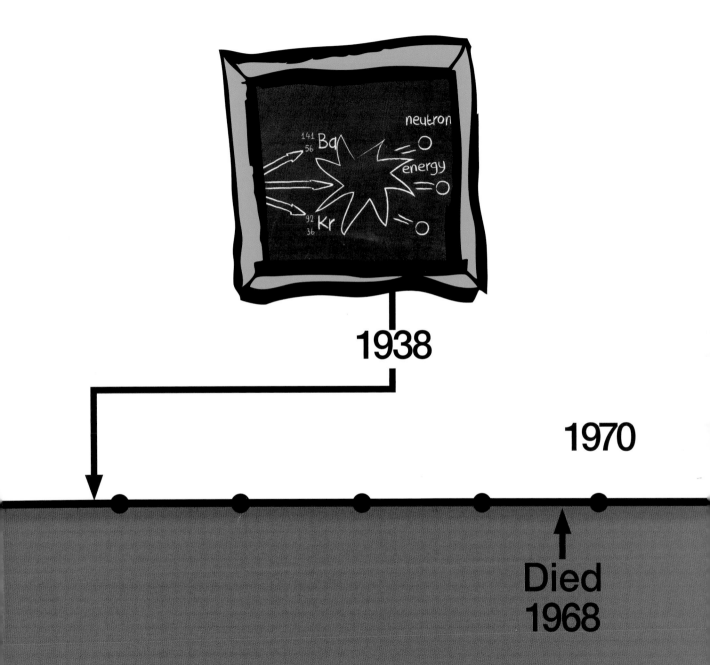

1938

1970

Died
1968

glossary

atoms (AT-uhmz) the tiniest parts of elements

doctorate (DAHK-tur-et) the highest degree (or title) that a student can earn at a university

energy (EN-ur-jee) power from coal, electricity, or other sources that makes machines work and produces heat

physics (FIZ-iks) the science that studies light, heat, sound, electricity, motion, and force

research (REE-surch) studying or gathering facts in a certain field, usually to learn more or to solve a problem

tutored (TOO-turhd) taught by a teacher who gives private lessons to one or a few students at a time

weapons (WEP-uhnz) objects used in fighting or hunting

index